From Betrayal to Breakthrough

A Journey of Healing, Faith, and Finding Myself

Wanna Perkins

ISBN: 979-8-218-79505-4
Published by Wanna Perkins
Printed in the United States of America

"The Lord is close to the brokenhearted and saves those who are crushed in spirit."

— Psalm 34:18

Table of Contents

Acknowledgments

No journey is ever walked alone, and this book is no exception.

To my family and friends, thank you for your prayers, encouragement, and unwavering support. Every kind word, every prayer, every listening ear carried me further than you will ever know.

A special thank you to my cousin Vameker, who walked beside me through the process of writing this book. Thank you for reading drafts, giving feedback, and helping me see what to add, what to take out, and what sounded right. Your honesty, patience, and love helped shape these pages into what they are now.

To the women of Fallbrook Women's Ministry, you never knew what I was going through during those Bible studies, but your fellowship was a lifeline to me in ways I cannot describe. Thank you for showing me the power of community and sisterhood in Christ.

To the women in my Facebook group, who prayed with me and stood with me even though we were strangers, you became sisters. You reminded me that I was not alone in the fight for healing.

To the students I cared for as a school nurse, you never knew how much you gave me during that time. Your joy and love reminded me that life still had beauty, even when I felt empty.

And to my sons, my rocks, my motivation, my greatest blessings. Thank you for loving me through it all. Thank you for your patience as I found my way, and for reminding me daily of why I keep pushing forward. Your words, "Mom, I'm proud of you," are treasures I will carry forever.

Finally, I want to acknowledge the breaking itself, the heartbreak, the tears, the moments that nearly crushed me. Without them, I wouldn't be able to tell this story, and I wouldn't be the woman I am becoming. Every trial gave birth to a testimony worth sharing. For that, I am even thankful for the pain, because God used it to reveal His purpose.

Author's Note

To the one holding this book, You are seen, you are loved.

Maybe you're walking through betrayal. Maybe you're sitting in the ashes of what was. Maybe you're silently wondering if you'll ever feel whole again.

From Betrayal to Breakthrough is not just about me telling my story, but was written to remind you that God sees yours too.

This book was born from real pain, real prayer, and real healing. I cried in bathroom stalls. I worshipped through heartbreak. I found strength on quiet Vermont mornings and gym floors during prep for my first competition. I carried grief, but I also found grace.

And somewhere along the way, I realized this wasn't just about loss, it was about becoming. You are not alone. You are not too broken. And you are not forgotten. God can still write beauty into your story, just like He did mine.

So, take your time with these pages. Breathe. Reflect. Cry if you need to. Laugh if you can. And know that this story was written with you in mind.

With love and healing,

Wanna Perkins

Prologue

Red Flags & Free Will

I always knew something wasn't right. There were signs, early ones. Subtle ones. Loud ones. But they were all there. The foundation wasn't solid. The peace wasn't present. And deep down, I felt it.

From the beginning, I would pray, "God, if he's not for me, show me." And every single time, God did.

He showed me in conversations that didn't sit well in my spirit. He showed me in the lack of emotional safety.

He showed me through chaos that came disguised as love.

But I didn't listen. I wasn't ready to let go. I confused potential with purpose. I thought maybe if I just prayed harder, loved deeper, stayed longer… it would fix itself.

The thing about God is, He's so loving, He doesn't force us. He gives us free will. He lets us choose. He lets us walk paths that detour us just to bring us back wiser. And I bumped my head more times than I want to admit.

I stayed in a cycle because it was familiar. I ignored the flags because I wanted the fantasy. And yet, with every tear I cried, God wasn't punishing me, He was protecting me, positioning me, preparing me for truth. And with all those red flags, I still went on to get married.

I remember pacing back and forth in the bridal suite of the church, torn and anxious. I didn't feel peace. I felt pressure. I kept wishing I had my car keys. He had sent a limo to pick me up, which meant I had no way out. And I remember thinking, if I had my keys, I would leave. I would've been a runaway bride. But I didn't.

I walked down that aisle anyway, not because I was certain, but because I was scared. Scared of embarrassment. Scared of disappointing people who had come to witness a wedding, not a cancellation. I felt like backing out would make me a failure. But the irony?

I still ended up facing embarrassment, only now it was public and painful, wrapped in the word divorce. Looking back, I don't beat myself up. I now understand that grace covers even my stubbornness. That sometimes, lessons have to be lived before they can be learned.

"There is a way that appears to be right, but in the end it leads to death." (Proverbs 14:12, NIV)

God was never absent. He was always whispering, always warning, and always waiting. Waiting for me to finally believe what He already knew. That I was worthy of more. That I didn't have to force what was never meant. That His *"no"* was His mercy, not rejection.

Now I look back at those red flags not with shame, but with revelation. They were not just warnings, they were invitations. Invitations to trust Him. Invitations to choose me. Invitations to break free from the bondage of settling.

And now, I don't just thank God for the blessings. I thank Him for the blocks. I thank Him for every unanswered prayer that protected me. I thank Him for every red flag that finally turned into my green light to walk away.

Because the truth is:

Sometimes the most loving thing God can do is let us bump our heads. Until we realize that His way is the only way that leads to peace.

CHAPTER 1

When the Ground Shakes

It was a regular day at school. I was in my nurse's office, tending to children with scraped knees and upset stomachs, the usual. Then my phone rang. It was my husband. He didn't sound like himself. He hesitated, then said it: *"I love someone else."* And, just like that, my world cracked open.

I froze. My heart dropped into my stomach. I couldn't breathe, let alone process what he just said. I don't even remember hanging up the phone. I just remember standing there, stunned, as the floor beneath me felt like it was disappearing. I rushed to the bathroom, locked the door, and wept. The kind of weeping where your body shakes and there are no words, just groans from deep inside your soul. I tried to pull myself together, splash some water on my face. I had students depending on me. I had to show up. I had to be "Nurse Wanna." But that day, I wasn't okay.

I thought I had hidden it so well, my tears, my trembling hands. But one of my students came in and looked at me closely. She said, "Nurse, are you okay?" I forced a smile and said, "Oh, I have allergies." She left, and I thought that was the end of it. But she came back a few minutes later holding something in her hand. It was a Bible.

Of all the things she could have brought—tissues, a note, even just a hug, she brought a Bible. It was as if she was saying, without words: *"I see your pain. And I know Who can hold it."*

I stood there staring at it for a second, almost too broken to reach out and take it. But when I did, my hands trembled, not from weakness, but from the overwhelming sense that God was reaching for *me* through that child. Through her innocence. Through her faith. Through her *boldness*.

How could someone so young be so in tune with what my heart desperately needed? I hadn't prayed yet. I hadn't said His name. I was still too stunned, too wounded. But there He was, already present in my pain. Already working. Already whispering: *"I'm still here."*

Have you ever had a moment like that? One where, even in your most broken state, God sent a gentle reminder that He hadn't forgotten you? Maybe it was a song on the radio, a friend's unexpected text, a verse you hadn't read in years suddenly speaking straight to your ache.

That Bible in her little hands was a divine interruption. A holy gesture. It reminded me that even when betrayal blindsides you and your whole world caves in, God is never far. He sees the tears you cry behind closed doors. He hears the groans that words can't carry. And sometimes, often in the quietest, most surprising ways,

He sends someone to remind you: *you are not alone.*

That child couldn't have known the depth of what I was going through. But God did. And through her, He reminded me that He was near. Closer than the next breath. Holding space for my grief, even when I couldn't hold myself together.

She opened it up, turned to Psalm 34:18, and began to read.

"The Lord is close to the brokenhearted and saves those who are crushed in spirit." Right there, in that moment, I broke again, but not from pain. This time, it was from God's nearness.

It was as if those words reached past my tears, past my confusion, past my shattered heart, and wrapped themselves around me like a warm blanket. I was familiar with that verse but, never had it felt so *personal*. To this very day, I have no idea if she knows how much her voice was carrying the weight of heaven but, what I do know is, God was in that room.

His nearness was not just a concept anymore; it became a reality I could feel. I wasn't alone in that nurse's office. I wasn't abandoned in my grief. God was right there, sitting in the silence, resting beside me in the stillness. I could feel Him closer than the very breath in my lungs, closer than the pounding of my broken heart.

It wasn't the kind of closeness where everything suddenly felt better. It was deeper than that. It was the kind of presence that doesn't rush to fix you, but simply *sits with you*. That day, I didn't need answers. I didn't even need words. I just needed to feel that someone, *He* was with me. And He was.

If you've ever been so crushed that you couldn't form the words to pray, so undone that you didn't know how to ask for help, let me tell you from my experience, *God is still near.* He doesn't require a perfect prayer or a polished faith to come close. In fact, it's your brokenness that draws Him in.

The nearness of God isn't just poetic. It's not reserved for Sunday morning services. It shows up in silent car rides, in tear-stained pillows and may even show up in an elementary school clinic office when your world has just fallen apart and all you can do is weep behind a locked door.

God's nearness holds space for sorrow. He doesn't flinch at your pain. He doesn't walk away when the wound is too deep or the betrayal too great. He leans in. He surrounds. He *stays.* I felt Him that day, in that moment, in the quiet courage of a child holding a Bible. He wasn't distant, cold, or silent.

Whatever you're carrying, however hidden your heartbreak may be, God sees it. He knows. And He *is not far.* He draws near to us when we're weary, when we're broken, when we're doing our best to smile on the outside while falling apart on the inside.

Psalms 34:18 wasn't just read over me; it was *spoken into me.* Into the shattered places of my heart and the hollow silence of my soul. It didn't take away the pain, but it reminded me of something even more powerful: *God hadn't left me in it.* He came closer. He always does.

Out of all the ways God could've comforted me, He sent a child. A child who saw through the mask I was wearing. A child who brought me a Word from heaven when I had no strength to seek it for myself. I sat there stunned, tears pouring down my face again, but this time, they weren't just tears of grief. They were tears of being seen.

God saw me in that bathroom; in the middle of heartbreak and in my weakest moment whispered, *"I'm still here."*

CHAPTER 2

Praying for the Wrong Thing

After that life-altering phone call, I spiraled into a place that felt like desperation mixed with unwavering faith. It was as if my soul had been cracked open, and in the rawness of my pain, I began to cry out to God in ways I never had before. I became a prayer warrior, not in title, but in truth. I found myself on my knees, in the car, in the shower, and awake in the dark hours of the night, whispering and sometimes wailing prayers into the silence. I didn't care where I was; I just needed to reach God. I fasted earnestly, denying myself food as a physical expression of my spiritual hunger for God to intervene. I wasn't just praying, I was pleading. My heart was desperate for Him to fix my marriage, to bring my husband home, to breathe life into what had died. I believed so deeply in the power of restoration that I told God I was willing to do anything if He would just make it right again.

In my pursuit, I discovered *Rejoice Marriage Ministries,* and their daily devotionals became like manna in the wilderness. Each word nourished my faith and gave me just enough strength to believe one more day. I devoured testimonies from women whose husbands had returned after betrayal, infidelity, even remarriage.

Their stories lit a flicker of hope in me. I thought to myself, "God, if You did it for them, You can do it for me." Hebrews 13:8 reminded me, *"Jesus Christ is the same yesterday and today and forever."* If He was capable of restoring their marriages, surely mine was not beyond His reach.

I bought every book I could find on prayer, fasting, and spiritual warfare. I listened to CDs filled with scripture, declarations, and encouragement, letting them play on loop in my home like a soundtrack of hope. I anointed the doorposts of my house with oil, symbolically marking it as a place of faith and promise, just as the Israelites did in Exodus 12 during Passover. I went to war in the spirit, fighting not just for my marriage, but for what I believed was God's will. Ephesians 6:12 came alive to me: *"For we wrestle not against flesh and blood, but against principalities, against powers… against spiritual wickedness in high places."*

And deep within me, no matter how much time passed, a small ember of hope remained lit. I still longed for that moment when he would return, confess that it had all been a mistake, and choose me again. I hoped God would rewrite the ending in a way that looked like reconciliation.

But then, something unexpected began to happen. Slowly and painfully, I began to realize that this wasn't just about my marriage. I was focused on my husband and God was focused on *me*.

He started peeling back layers I didn't even know I had. Pride. Control. Fear of abandonment. Deep insecurities that had long been buried beneath the roles I carried "wife," "mother," "helper." These titles, while beautiful, had become a mask for the brokenness I had ignored. I was so consumed with fixing the external, our relationship, our family, our image, that I hadn't noticed how deeply wounded I was internally. Psalm 139:23-24 became my reality: *"Search me, God, and know my heart; test me and know my anxious thoughts. See if there is any offensive way in me, and lead me in the way everlasting."*

During one of my fasts, when I was still desperately seeking answers, I heard a whisper in my spirit: "You're praying for the wrong thing." I froze in stillness. My heart pounded. "What do You mean, Lord?" I asked. "I'm praying for my marriage... for my family... for my covenant." And then, in His gentle and loving way, God spoke again: "You're praying for restoration... but I'm trying to heal *you*."

That moment shifted everything. It was as if a veil had been lifted. My prayers began to change, from "Lord, bring him home," to "Lord, bring *me* home, back to who You created me to be." I wasn't just asking for my husband anymore, I was asking for my identity. I wanted to remember the woman I was before heartbreak, before betrayal, before I gave so much of myself away that I didn't recognize my own reflection. I longed to return to the daughter God had designed, the one not defined by marital status or circumstances, but by His love.

There were still days when I wept bitterly for my marriage. Nights when the ache of hope unfulfilled pressed heavy on my chest. I still had faith that things *could* change. But slowly, my heart began to shift. My confidence wasn't in the outcome anymore;

it was in the One who held the outcome. I started to believe that even if the story didn't unfold the way I wanted, God would still be good. He would still be healer. He would still be restorer.

Joel 2:25 echoed in my spirit: *"I will restore to you the years that the locust hath eaten."* Maybe, just maybe, restoration wouldn't look like my husband returning. Maybe it wouldn't be the fairytale ending I had envisioned. Perhaps God's restoration would look like reconciliation with *myself*. With the woman I had forgotten. With the purpose I had put on the shelf. With the love of a Father who had never stopped chasing after me, even when I was only chasing after someone else.

CHAPTER 3

Coping in the Dark

When Healing Isn't Holy

Healing is not linear. It's not always neat, tidy, or graceful. Sometimes, healing looks like a mess. And I've learned—sometimes the hard way—that when you're hurting, you'll reach for almost anything just to feel okay, even if it's just for a moment.

After the divorce, I was overwhelmed by silence—not just in my home, but in my soul. The kind of silence that once held the presence of another person, even if that person wasn't good for me. The quiet became deafening. And in the absence of what was familiar, I filled the space with distractions.

Friends would say, "Girl, it's time to date again," and at first, I resisted. I knew I wasn't ready. But eventually, I gave in. I downloaded the dating apps, not because I was healed, not because I was whole, but because I wanted attention. I craved validation. I just wanted to feel seen.

If I'm being honest, I had a little roster—five to seven people I talked to regularly. Late-night conversations, playful flirting, a few dates here and there. And while some moments felt fun and exciting, they were just temporary highs. Because once the call ended, the date was over, or the dopamine wore off, the emptiness returned—heavier and louder than before. I was still broken. Still grieving. Still mourning the version of life I thought I'd have.

That's when I started slipping into situationships. These weren't connections built on love or purpose, but on pain, loneliness, and unresolved trauma. Some of those situations turned physical, and I told myself it was harmless. Maybe even empowering. Maybe it would make me feel desired, connected—maybe even healed. But it didn't. The physical satisfaction was fleeting. The emotional and spiritual aftermath lingered far longer than the moment ever did. I felt shame. I felt regret. I felt like I was slowly losing parts of myself.

In that low place, I started exploring things I normally wouldn't. I dabbled in tarot cards and New Age practices. I tried manifesting peace, burned sage, looked into crystals—anything to feel in control or make sense of what God was—or wasn't—doing in my life. I was desperate for answers, for clarity, for something that would quiet the chaos. But none of it worked. Nothing filled the God-shaped void inside me.

Looking back, I see it now: by stepping outside of God's will—even just to cope—I opened doors that ultimately delayed my healing. I thought I was finding comfort, but what I was actually doing was compounding my pain. I gave people access to my heart, my bed, and my mind who were never meant to be there, all because I didn't want to feel alone. But the truth is, distractions delay deliverance. The more I tried to distract myself from the pain, the more untangling God had to do later to restore me. And the beautiful part? He still did it anyway.

It wasn't until I grew tired—tired of being tired, tired of fake connections, tired of feeling emptier after every temporary high— that I realized I didn't want another man's number. I wanted peace. I didn't want a text back. I wanted wholeness. So, I returned to the only source that had ever given me real healing—God.

When everything in my world felt like it was crumbling, I needed somewhere to go, somewhere to run. I wasn't looking for answers as much as I was searching for air. I needed emotional and spiritual outlets; lifelines I could cling to when I felt like I was drowning. And so, I found myself chasing avenues—not physical places, but sacred spaces. Places where hope flickered, even if faintly.

I started journaling again. I opened my Bible. I Googled scriptures about strength, heartbreak, and forgiveness. Slowly, I began to see that everything I had been chasing in people, practices, and pleasure was already in His Word. Everything I needed was there all along.

CHAPTER 4

Sacred Spaces

As I leaned into the rediscovery of truth—through journaling, through scripture, through simply being still—I began to notice a shift. Healing didn't come all at once, but it started to feel real, even in small moments. God wasn't just calling me to stop running from the pain; He was inviting me to rest in Him. I needed more than just insight—I needed safe, sacred spaces to breathe, to process, to *be*. Not physical escapes, but spiritual sanctuaries where I could meet God, even in the mess. And that's when I realized: healing also happens in the spaces we create to hold it.

I turned to *Rejoice Marriage Ministries*, desperate for insight, for clarity, for anything that might help me hold on. I consumed everything they offered—books, devotionals, testimonies of prodigal spouses returning home after infidelity, remarriage, or abandonment. I wanted that to be *my* story. I wanted to believe that restoration wasn't just possible—it was promised. I wasn't just hoping. I was fighting. Fasting. Praying. Pleading.

In my search for community, I joined Facebook groups filled

with women who were also standing for their marriages. Women who, like me, were praying for their husbands to come home. We became warriors in the comments—encouraging one another, lifting each other up with scripture, crying together across digital spaces. There was a raw beauty in our unity, a sense of sisterhood built not on success, but on shared suffering and steadfast hope.

But the truth? Every single one of us got divorced.

Still, we check in from time to time. There's something about walking through the fire together that forms a bond nothing can break. A strange sisterhood born from disappointment, yes—but also from divine perseverance.

And then there were the **YouTube sermons.** I would play them for hours, letting voices of faith echo through my home—messages on covenant, on restoration, on forgiveness and endurance. These sermons became my spiritual soundtrack. But every time one of them touched the subject of "release," "separation," or "letting go," something inside me would twist. My stomach would knot. I'd cry—deep, aching sobs—because I couldn't bear the thought. Letting go felt like losing. It felt like failure.

I didn't want to be another divorce statistic. Not another broken branch on a family tree already full of fractures. Not after my mother and stepfather. Not after my grandparents. *Not me.* I had convinced myself that I was meant to break the generational curse. And if I just prayed hard enough, believed long enough, held on tight enough, God would fix it. So, I clung harder.

I kept most of it to myself. I didn't talk deeply to many friends. I smiled when I needed to, wore strength like makeup, and performed normalcy with practiced ease. Because I didn't want anyone to really see me breaking. Vulnerability felt too dangerous. Too raw. And truthfully, I didn't think I'd survive if I let it all spill out.

Instead, I turned to *safe places*, family members and, sometimes, complete strangers who didn't carry the weight of expectation. They didn't expect me to be strong. They just let me be.

I called my aunt—not the one who preaches, but the one who *prays*. The one who loves hard, without judgment. I didn't want clichés or churchy responses. I wanted comfort. But she gave me something better: **truth**. She saw beyond the heartbreak, past the desperation, and spoke directly to my worth. She didn't soften her words to make them easier to hear, but she wrapped them in love. And though I wasn't ready to receive it all in the moment, her voice planted seeds that would later bloom into freedom.

And then there was **my uncle**—God bless him. That man called me *every single morning* for a month, just to pray with me. Not to fix things, not to offer opinions, but simply to cover me. He gave me spiritual armor when I couldn't dress myself. His voice became a steady reassurance that God was still with me, even when I felt completely alone.

My mother... she did what she could. But I didn't tell her everything. Not because I didn't trust her, but because I was afraid. When you're still holding onto hope for reconciliation, it's hard to share the whole truth. You fear that if you forgive, she won't. That if you ever found your way back to healing—especially with the person who hurt you—your family might never see him the same again. That tension is heavy. It's a silent grief all its own.

Through it all, I tried to protect **my sons.** I didn't want them to carry my pain. I didn't want them to see their mother shattered. I wanted to be brave for them—even when I didn't feel brave myself. So, I showed up, held my head high, and did the best I could. Because sometimes being brave doesn't mean you feel strong. It just means you don't quit.

"The righteous cry out, and the Lord hears them; he delivers them from all their troubles. The Lord is close to the brokenhearted and saves those who are crushed in spirit." **(Psalm 34:17–18, NIV)**

I was broken. But I wasn't abandoned. Even in my silence, God heard every cry. Every whisper. Every "why."

Those avenues I ran to—ministries, devotionals, prayer calls, strangers, scriptures—they didn't save my marriage. But they *did* help save *me.* They didn't remove the storm, but they held me steady in it. They reminded me that I wasn't alone. They became places of refuge when I didn't feel safe in my own story. They helped carry me when I couldn't walk on my own. They gave me spiritual oxygen when I was gasping for breath.

And now, as I look back, I don't thank God for the pain—but I do thank Him for the provision. For the voices He sent. For the spaces where I could unravel without shame. For the prayers that became a lifeline when I couldn't pray for myself.

This was the chapter where I learned something sacred:

You don't have to hold it all together to be held by God.

CHAPTER 5

The Mask Had to Fall

For the longest time, I wore a mask—not a physical one, but a carefully curated version of myself. The version that looked strong. Unbothered. In control. The version that smiled in pictures, posted scriptures, quoted healing words, and gave the illusion that everything was okay. But the truth? I was falling apart inside.

I wanted to control the narrative. I didn't want anyone to see my pain. I wanted people to believe I had it all together.

Because if they believed it, maybe I could too.

But healing doesn't happen behind a mask. And masks, no matter how convincing, eventually crack.

The cracks came quickly when everything spilled out onto social media. When his posts made our private pain public. When the truth I tried so hard to hide became the story everyone whispered about. Suddenly, I was no longer the one managing the narrative. I was no longer in control. I was exposed.

I had to live in the tension of being publicly embarrassed, privately broken, and still expected to show up like nothing had happened. I was cheated on. Humiliated. The kind of betrayal that you don't just feel—you carry it. In your body. In your silence. In your smile that doesn't quite reach your eyes anymore.

And yet, it was in *that* exposure—raw and painful—that God started to do something deeper.

I couldn't fake it anymore. I couldn't perform healing like it was a stage act. I had to actually *walk through it.*

When the mask came off, I finally met myself—the real me. The hurting me. The woman who had spent years hiding behind strength and perfection. The woman who had held in tears during meetings and smiled through heartbreak. The woman who was exhausted from pretending. And yet, the woman God still loved. Not the curated version, not the polished image. Just me. Stripped down, vulnerable, bare. Without performance. Without pretending. Without makeup, filters, or facades.

"You will know the truth, and the truth will set you free." (John 8:32, NIV)

And the truth? It was hard. But it was also holy.

God didn't need my pretend strength. He needed my surrendered heart.

Through the shame, He showed me grace. Through the embarrassment, He reminded me of my worth. Through the raw, unfiltered truth, He met me with healing.

It was in that place of complete honesty—no more hiding, no more pretending—that He started rebuilding me. But it wasn't easy. I had to learn how to stop explaining myself to people who would never understand my choices or my pain. I had to stop shrinking to make others comfortable with my healing journey.

I walked with God through a season where silence became my best protection, and solitude became my safest place. I cried in the shower, worshipped in my car, journaled through sleepless nights, and showed up to work like nothing was wrong. But something *was* wrong. Something deep. And I was finally brave enough to admit it.

Here's the truth: the mask didn't protect me. It trapped me. It trapped me in people's opinions. It trapped me in shame. It trapped me in silence. But God broke the silence. He shattered the shame. He helped me break free. The breaking became the breakthrough. And the mask had to fall so the healing could rise.

So, if you're reading this while wearing a mask—if you're hiding, performing, or carrying the crushing weight of people's expectations—I want you to know something:

You don't have to be perfect to be powerful. You don't have to hide to be holy. And you don't have to wear a mask to be loved.

Let it fall. Let God meet you in what's real. That's where the healing begins.

CHAPTER 6

Beauty for Ashes

After the divorce, I did something that most people would probably consider wild, unexpected, even outrageous. I booked a divorce photoshoot. Yes, you read that right. And in that moment, it felt incredibly right. I wasn't looking for attention or trying to stir controversy. What I was doing was deeply personal, symbolic, and necessary for my healing journey. I allowed myself to go through all the stages, grief, anger, release, and this photoshoot became a part of that process. It wasn't just about capturing images; it was about reclaiming a part of myself that had been buried under sorrow and disappointment.

For the shoot, I took my wedding dress, once pristine, white, and full of hope, and I deliberately stained it brown. I splattered red paint across the fabric, representing the brokenness and pain that had pierced my heart. I even crafted a bloody heart as a visual expression of the anguish I had carried inside. It was raw. It was emotional. It was symbolic of the shattered covenant, the deep wound of betrayal, and the slow, painful bleed of dreams that never got fulfilled. My photographer, Heather, brought the entire concept to life with sensitivity and brilliance. The theme was "Murder the Dress." To some, that might sound aggressive or extreme, but to me, it was sacred. It was something I *needed* to do, not for revenge, not to pretend the pain wasn't real, but to confront it head-on.

This act was not a delusion or denial. I didn't do it to erase the reality of my pain or minimize what had happened. I did it because I needed to reclaim something that had been stripped away from me: my worth. Somewhere along the way, in the midst of the heartbreak, betrayal, and unraveling of my marriage, I had forgotten how deeply valuable I still was, not because of someone else's love, but because of who I was in God. Some people looked at the photos and thought it was strange. Others said it looked like I was mourning. A few assumed I was acting out of bitterness or spite. But none of them knew the spiritual battle I had been fighting behind the scenes.

To me, this wasn't just a photoshoot, it was a declaration of spiritual warfare. This was not about vanity or visibility. It was about power, about standing in the authority God had given me as His daughter and refusing to let the story end in shame. When I wore that dress, broken and stained as it was, I felt something I hadn't felt in a long time: wholeness. I felt worthy. I felt *chosen*. Not by a man, but by God Himself. It was my way of saying, "This is not where the story ends. I may have been rejected by one, but I am still accepted by the One who matters most." Ephesians 1:4 reminds us, *"He chose us in Him before the creation of the world to be holy and blameless in His sight."* That truth became my anchor.

Wearing that torn and painted wedding dress became a prophetic act. It was a symbol that even though someone else may have discarded the covenant, God still held me together. It was my way of declaring that the betrayal wouldn't define me. That even if someone else couldn't see my beauty, I still carried it. That even if my earthly marriage had ended, I was still the bride of Christ. Isaiah 54:5 says, *"For your Maker is your husband, the Lord Almighty is his name."* That verse reminded me that I was never truly abandoned, I was held.

And then, that same week, something else happened. One day, I was outside, simply walking, trying to breathe deeply and keep my spirit intact. Life felt fragile, but I was holding on. As I looked up at the sky, I saw it: a rainbow. At first, it was faint, almost hidden behind the clouds. I didn't even realize I had taken a picture of it until later, but there it was, God's promise stretched across the sky. In that quiet moment, I felt the whisper of heaven. It was a reminder that storms don't last forever. That beauty still breaks through clouds. That no matter how dark the past had been, light was on the other side.

That rainbow became a sacred symbol for me, just like the photos. It wasn't just about what I had lost, but about what God was beginning to rebuild. It wasn't about heartbreak anymore; it was about healing. It was about the fulfillment of Isaiah 61:3, which says, *"To all who mourn...He will give a crown of beauty for ashes, a joyous blessing instead of mourning, festive praise instead of despair."* That verse wasn't just words on a page; it was my reality. God was giving me beauty for ashes. He was trading my despair for joy, my brokenness for something far more whole.

We often talk about closure like it's a conversation, like it's something someone else gives us when they apologize or explain why they hurt us. But sometimes, closure is something entirely different. Sometimes, closure is a stained dress. Sometimes it's a rainbow hidden in the clouds. Sometimes it's a photo that speaks louder than words ever could. And sometimes, closure is simply a whisper from God that says: *"You're not forgotten. I'm still writing your story."*

CHAPTER 7

Losing Weight & Gaining Strength

The divorce didn't just wreck me emotionally; it wrecked me physically. It's hard to describe the kind of toll that grief takes on the body, but I felt it in every cell. I had carried the weight of so many things for so long: the weight of responsibility, of being the glue that held everything together. I had worn the invisible burdens of stress, anxiety, and disappointment like armor, trying to shield everyone else while silently breaking down on the inside. I smiled when I was crumbling. I showed up when I wanted to hide. I held my family together while silently falling apart. And all of that weight? It didn't just stay in my heart, it showed up on my face, on my hips, and deep in my spirit. I was exhausted from carrying it all.

But then something shifted. Something awakened in me the day I decided to train for a bodybuilding competition. At first glance, it may have seemed superficial, something people associate with vanity or attention. But for me, it was nothing of the sort. It wasn't about trying to look good for anyone else, and it certainly wasn't about revenge. It was about something far more sacred: reclaiming *me*. I needed something to focus on. I needed something that wasn't about saving someone else or holding together a crumbling relationship. I needed to know what it would feel like to pour all of that energy, discipline, commitment, control, into *myself* for once.

For the first time in years, I wasn't managing someone else's emotions or trying to fix what wasn't mine to fix. I wasn't shrinking myself to keep the peace or stretching myself thin just to keep someone else comfortable. I was investing in my own healing, building something solid, something lasting, within me. The weight began to fall away, but not just the physical kind. I started shedding the invisible burdens that had clung to me for far too long.

I lost the weight of grief, the constant ache of what could've been. I lost the weight of guilt, the voices that told me I should've done more. I lost the weight of shame, the heavy cloak I wore when I asked myself, over and over again, "Why wasn't I enough?"

With every rep I pushed through, every mile I ran, every clean meal I prepared, I was declaring something powerful: *"I'm still here."* I wasn't disappearing, I was reappearing. I was coming back to life.

One of the most profound parts of this journey was the way my sons watched it all unfold. They saw more than their mother getting in shape, they saw their mother *transform.* They witnessed resilience. And that, more than anything, became my real motivation. I didn't want my boys to see a woman broken by betrayal; I wanted them to see a woman rebuilding from the ashes. I wanted them to know what it looks like when someone gets knocked down and still chooses to rise. I wanted to show them that strength doesn't always look like fighting battles, it sometimes looks like healing from them. I wanted to teach them that self-worth isn't defined by who stays or who walks away. It's found in how we respond when the world around us crumbles. It's in how we rebuild, brick by brick, prayer by prayer.

The day of the competition came. I stood on that stage in full glam, tan skin, sparkly bikini, lashes done to perfection, but the real glow wasn't what anyone could see on the outside. It radiated from within. It came from the grit that got me out of bed when I didn't want to move. It came from the grace that covered me when I felt weak. It came from the quiet, inner strength that God had been growing in me the entire time. That stage wasn't about showcasing my body, it was about honoring my battle. It was about standing tall in front of the world and saying, *"I didn't quit."*

I didn't win a trophy that day. But I won something far greater. I won *me* back.

I was reminded of the verse from Proverbs 31:25: *"She is clothed with strength and dignity, and she laughs without fear of the future."* That scripture became my anthem. I was no longer living under the weight of shame or sorrow. I was clothed in strength. Dignity had replaced despair. I could laugh again, not because life was perfect, but because I was no longer afraid of what came next. I was no longer defined by the ashes of what had burned down. I was defined by the beauty that was rising in its place.

Because I wasn't just shedding pounds. I was shedding the past.

CHAPTER 8

Vermont & The Mirror

After the whirlwind of heartbreak, betrayal, and emotional chaos, I realized what my soul needed most wasn't answers, closure, or even restoration. I needed quiet. I needed stillness, something I hadn't felt in what seemed like years. In the wake of so much noise, internal and external, I longed for a place where I could simply *breathe*. So, I did something bold. I took a travel nurse contract in Vermont, a state I had never visited, surrounded by people I didn't know, far away from anything familiar. No family. No friends. No history to remind me of what had been lost. No distractions to mask the ache.

It was just the mountains, my assignments, and God.

For the first time in a long time, I found myself alone. Not just in the physical sense, but emotionally and spiritually, too. There was no one to perform for, no one to rescue, no one to impress or convince that I was okay. I didn't have to wear a mask. I didn't have to hold anyone else up. And in that silence, pure, undisturbed quiet, I was forced to finally face *myself*.

I remember one particular moment that changed everything. I stood in front of the mirror, bare-faced, no makeup, no distractions, no filter. Just me. Just raw, uncovered truth. And I looked at myself with a clarity I hadn't had in years. I whispered aloud, "You're still here." And I didn't say it in defeat. I didn't say it in despair. I said it as a *declaration*. A victory cry. I had survived the breaking. Now, it was time to embrace the *becoming*.

Vermont held a kind of sacredness I hadn't expected. The air was crisp and intentional, like it had something to teach me. The mountains didn't ask about my pain or my past, they just stood tall and steady, unmoved by human drama. And somehow, in their quiet strength, they reminded me that I could stand tall, too. The trees didn't shrink in the winter or apologize for their barrenness. They simply *were*—rooted, enduring. They became symbols of quiet resilience.

By day, I worked, focusing on my patients and fulfilling my purpose as a nurse. But it was outside of work where the deeper healing happened. I worshipped in my car, letting praise songs become my lifeline. I cried on long walks through the woods, letting tears fall freely in the safety of solitude. I journaled late into the night, pouring my thoughts onto paper like a conversation between my heart and heaven.

It wasn't until I had true silence that I realized how loud my life had been. The emotional noise I had been living with, the questions, the loops, the false hope—was deafening. I no longer had to wrestle with, "What did he say?" or, "Is he coming home?" or, "Should I call him?" That constant mental clutter was gone.

And in its place was something rare and sacred: *just me and God.*

And that… that's when the *real* healing began.

There's something about silence that amplifies the soul. When the world grows quiet, the noise inside of you finally rises to the surface—and you're forced to listen. In that stillness, God began to whisper things I had been too distracted—or too afraid—to hear back home. He began to gently peel back layers I thought I had already dealt with. He showed me areas where bitterness still lingered. He introduced me to the little girl inside—the one who felt abandoned, not just by a man, but by life itself. And in His mercy, He didn't stop at exposure. He began to *rebuild.*

With each day that passed, I felt something shifting within me. I was becoming stronger—but not the kind of strength the world often glorifies. This wasn't about plastering on a smile or pushing through in denial. This was a sacred strength—a strength rooted in surrender. A strength born from rest. From release. From learning to let go and let God truly carry the weight. Isaiah 30:15 says, *"In quietness and trust is your strength."* That became my reality.

Vermont wasn't just a change in scenery. It was a *turning point.* A divine pause in the narrative of my life where God invited me to stop striving and start healing. Psalm 23:2–3 became my lifeline: *"He makes me lie down in green pastures, He leads me beside still waters, He restores my soul."* And truly, He did. He led me to still waters—not just outside, but within.

The mirror, once a painful reminder of all I'd lost, became

something new. It became my accountability—my place of honest reflection. But more than that, it became my *altar.* A place where I offered the broken pieces of my identity and invited God to transform them into something beautiful. I stopped looking for the woman I used to be—and started seeing the woman I was becoming.

CHAPTER 9

A Father's Wound and a Father's Love

I sat alone on the floor of my bedroom, back against the wall, the silence after my divorce papers were signed pressing in on me. My heart felt shattered not only by the end of my marriage, but by a deeper ache I hadn't expected. In that emptiness, I realized the pain cut into a far older scar – one formed in childhood, in the shape of my father. As I wept over my husband's betrayal, I sensed another voice of hurt inside, the voice of a little girl who felt abandoned and unloved. It was as if my divorce had pried open a door I had shut long ago, revealing unresolved grief I carried for years. I clung desperately to my faith in that dark moment, remembering that "The LORD is close to the brokenhearted and saves those who are crushed in spirit". In the stillness of that night, I whispered those ancient words, hoping they were true for me. I needed God's closeness more than ever, because I felt brokenhearted twice over – once as a wife, and once as a daughter.

The Hidden Wound

In the weeks after my marriage ended, waves of emotions washed over me that I struggled to understand. Yes, I was devastated by my husband's betrayal and the collapse of the life we built. But beneath that loss was a surprisingly familiar pain. It took me some time – and a lot of prayerful soul-searching, to realize that my ex-husband's abandonment had ripped the scab off a much older wound. I was not just mourning the loss of a spouse; I was reliving the unanswered tears of a little girl who used to wonder why her daddy wasn't there for her. The hidden wound of my childhood had reopened. Growing up, I had unmet expectations of my father that I learned to bury. He wasn't there for the day-to-day moments – the school recitals, the birthdays, the small triumphs and tears of my youth. I told myself I was "fine" and tried not to need him. But each time he forgot a promise or missed a milestone, a quiet voice inside me would whisper, "You weren't worth it to him." Over the years I built a wall around that voice, determined to be strong and not let the hurt show. I filled my life with achievements and later with a husband whom I hoped would always be by my side. I thought I had left the past in the past. Yet here I was, in my forties, facing an eerily similar heartbreak. My husband – the man who vowed "forever" – had left me, and with him went the future I dreamed of. In the aftermath, I felt exactly like that little girl again: not enough, easy to leave behind. The parallels were undeniable. One night, not long after the divorce was finalized, I dreamed of my father. In the dream I was a child waiting on the front steps of our house, waiting for him to come like he promised – but he never arrived. I woke up sobbing from that dream, the old disappointment as fresh as if it had just happened. All the feelings I had suppressed for years came rushing back: the feelings of abandonment, the anger at being left, the longing for a father's love that never quite materialized. It stunned me how strongly my soul still ached for Daddy. I realized that I had never truly healed from my father's absence; I had just learned to live with the wound. My divorce simply tore off the bandage. Suddenly I was grieving two losses – the end of my marriage and the fatherly love I never fully received. There were moments I sat with my journal, trying to sort out which tears were for my ex-husband and which were for my dad. Often, they intertwined. I wrote letters I never sent, addressed to my father: letters about a little girl's broken heart, about school awards he didn't see, and the empty seat at my college graduation. I admitted to myself that a part of me had always felt unworthy and unlovable because of his neglect – a lie that had quietly influenced my relationships, even my marriage. I had unconsciously feared my husband would abandon me, just as my father had. When it actually happened, that fear was confirmed in the worst way, and it hurt in a place I didn't even know I still had open. Amid this emotional turmoil, I found myself turning more earnestly to God. I had been a woman of faith for years, but this season drove me to a deeper dependency on my Heavenly Father. One afternoon I remember praying through sobs, "God, why does this hurt so much? Why do I feel like I'm losing my father all over again?" In that still, small moment, I sensed God tenderly revealing the truth: I needed to face the father-wound I'd buried. I sensed that this pain surfacing was not a punishment, but a process of purging – like an infection that needed to be cleaned so it could finally heal. It was as though

God was saying, now that it's open, let Me heal it. A scripture came to mind that gave me both comfort and pause: "Though my father and mother forsake me, the LORD will receive me."

I had read that verse many times before, but it struck me with new force. I truly felt forsaken by my earthly father – and now by my husband – but here was God's promise to receive me, to hold me close. I clung to that promise like a lifeline. In truth, I needed God to father me in this season, to fill the void left gaping in my chest. And slowly, I began to believe that He was indeed right there, ready to catch the daughter who felt so lost. In prayer, I even dared to voice my deepest hurts: "God, why didn't my dad love me the way I needed? Why wasn't I enough for him to stay?" I poured out years of disappointment and allowed myself to grieve openly before the Lord. Each tear felt like it washed another layer of hardened pain out of my heart. During this time, I also started to see my father with new eyes – eyes not only of a hurt daughter, but of a woman whom God was teaching about compassion and forgiveness. It wasn't an overnight change; it was gradual and often painful. I realized I had been carrying unforgiveness toward my dad in a hidden corner of my heart. I had walled it off, pretending it wasn't there, but it was poisoning me in subtle ways. Now, God was inviting me to open that door. I remembered how Jesus taught us to forgive others, and I read scriptures on forgiveness with a new perspective. One verse in particular convicted me: "Be kind and compassionate to one another, forgiving each other, just as in Christ God forgave you."

I had always known I should forgive, but now the call to forgive my father felt personal and urgent. How could I ask God to heal my heart if I was locking part of it away in bitterness?

A Journey Toward Forgiveness

Thus began a journey toward forgiveness and reconciliation that I never anticipated I would take so late in life. In prayer, I told God I was willing – willing to forgive my father, willing to try to reconcile – but I was also honest that I didn't know how. Memories of hurt don't just vanish overnight. Sometimes I would take one step forward (feeling mercy soften my heart) and then something would trigger me – an old family photo or a Father's Day card I never sent – and anger or sorrow would flood back in. It was a messy, non-linear process, but God was patient with me. I felt Him gently nudging me forward, reminding me how He had forgiven me of my own failings and how harboring resentment would only keep me trapped. On several occasions, I found myself in tears yet again, but these tears were cleansing. I would cry and pray, releasing a little more of the burden each time. During this season, I found unexpected comfort in the Bible's stories and promises about fatherhood. I took solace in knowing that God understood my pain – after all, Scripture describes Him as "a father to the fatherless"

And as I studied Jesus' life, I was moved by how He spoke of God as "Father" with such intimacy. It dawned on me that God's heart toward me was everything I had longed for in my earthly dad: protective, present, and full of unconditional love. That realization didn't erase my earthly hurt, but it gave me a foundation to stand on. I began to rest in the truth that I am deeply loved by my Heavenly Father, even if my earthly father's love had been flawed. This assurance gave me the strength to approach the next step: reaching out to my dad. I will never forget the day I decided to call him. It was a few months after my divorce was finalized. I had not spoken to my father in quite some time – our contact had dwindled to occasional holiday texts or third-hand updates through relatives. My hands were literally shaking as I dialed his number. I whispered a quick "Lord, help me do this in love" before I heard his voice answer, uncertain and a bit surprised to hear from me. After some polite catching up, I took a deep breath and told him honestly that my divorce had been very painful and had stirred up a lot of emotions from the past. My heart pounded as I explained, haltingly, that I realized I had been hurt by him leaving years ago more than I ever admitted. There was a pause – I could hear him exhale – and then he said quietly, "I'm so sorry." Those three words unlocked something in me. I hadn't called to demand an apology, but hearing them from my father, even softly and imperfectly, felt like cool water on a parched soul. My tears came then, a mix of sorrow and relief. "Dad, I forgive you," I sobbed out, barely able to speak. "I just… I want us to have a relationship, whatever that looks like. I don't want to carry this hurt anymore." What followed was one of the most honest conversations my father and I have ever had. It was as if years of pent-up words finally found their way out. He admitted that he knew he had fallen short as a father – he told me about the fear and shame he carried all these years for not being there. In that moment I saw not a villain who abandoned me, but a flawed man who had his own wounds and regrets. It didn't excuse the past, but it helped humanize him in my eyes. We talked for a long while, and though we didn't solve everything in one phone call, a foundation was laid. For the first time, we both truly acknowledged the pain between us. I told him about the little girl who used to watch the driveway, hoping to see his car pull up. He quietly said, "I wish I could go back and change things, but I can't. I hope you know how much I love you, in my own imperfect way." My heart cracked a little more – this time, in a good way, as the hardness started to break. After that day, my father and I began a delicate season of reconciliation. We spoke more frequently – brief calls or messages just to check in. At first it felt almost awkward, like learning a new dance, but gradually an authentic connection grew. I found myself praying for my dad often, not just that our relationship would heal, but that he would experience God's love and forgiveness in his own heart. There was a sweetness in praying for him; it further softened any remaining bitterness I had. I also noticed that as I forgave my father and let God heal that wound, I was simultaneously finding new strength to forgive my ex-husband for the divorce. The two journeys were strangely intertwined. My heart, once hardened by betrayal, was becoming tender again. The grace God gave me for my father overflowed to grace for my ex-husband. I realized forgiveness is not a one-time event but a lifestyle of continually releasing others from the debts of our hurt – just as God continually shows us mercy. Every time I chose to forgive, I was a little freer. It was fulfilling the scripture's call to forgive as Christ forgave me and in doing so, I was the one being set free. One scripture that I held onto tightly during this time was Romans 8:28 – "And we know that in all things God works for the good of those who love him, who have been called according to his purpose."

This verse became a beacon of hope for me. I began to see how God was indeed working "in all things" – even in my heartbreak – to bring about something good. It amazed me that God used the agony of my divorce to shine light on an older agony I had buried, so that He could heal me more completely. If you had told me a year earlier that anything good could come from the betrayal I endured, I would have struggled to believe it. But now I was witnessing a redemptive purpose unfold: my broken marriage drove me to address my broken childhood. In His mysterious way, God was weaving the strands of pain into a tapestry of healing.

Restored Hearts and Final Goodbyes

As winter melted into spring, I sensed a new peace sprouting in my heart. I was still navigating life as a single woman again, and I certainly had hard days of loneliness. But the heavy weight of bitterness was gone. In its place was a feeling of lightness – the result of forgiveness and God's comfort. My relationship with my father, though far from a storybook ideal, was improving. We even managed an in-person visit a couple of months after that pivotal phone call. I travelled to see him at his home, the first time I'd been there in years. I was nervous as I knocked on his door, but when he opened it, the smile and tear in his eye told me everything. He pulled me into a gentle hug, one that seemed to speak an unspoken apology and love all at once. I hugged him back, the little girl in me finally getting the embrace she had yearned for. We spent that afternoon looking through old photo albums he had kept. He showed me pictures of me as a toddler on his shoulders. I saw evidence that he cherished those memories, even if he hadn't been able to sustain our closeness. At one point, he sighed, "I missed so much… I'm sorry, sweetheart." I placed my hand on his and said, "We still have now, Dad. Let's make the most of it." It wasn't a dramatic moment, just a quiet agreement to move forward with grace. I silently thanked God for bringing us to this point – something I once thought impossible. As we parted that day, I told my father I loved him. It might have been the first time I initiated those words in adulthood. He looked a bit surprised, then replied softly, "I love you too, Wanna." I drove away with tears of gratitude streaming down my face, marveling at how far we had come in such a short time. Little did I know that God's timing was extraordinarily providential. Only a few months after that visit, my father passed away. When I got the call, I felt my stomach drop

In that moment, I was overwhelmed with gratitude that God had urged me to reconcile when He did. Had I waited or resisted, I might have lost the chance forever. Those next days all I could do was look back at text messages and the few pictures we got to take together.

I remembered Psalm 147:3: "He heals the brokenhearted and binds up their wounds."

It gave me comfort, reminding me that God was present, tending to my heart's wounds. I live with a regret. My dad called me, and I sent him to voicemail to talk to my mom. So, to deal with things, I imagine it was sometimes as if God's arms were wrapped around both of us – a father and daughter, and their Heavenly Father holding them together. "Thank you…for forgiving me," he managed to say. "You've given me a great gift, Wanna. I'm *at peace."* I choked back tears and told him I loved him, that there was nothing to forgive anymore – it was all in the past. "I love you, Dad," I said clearly, so he would have no doubt. He gave the faintest smile and murmured, "Love you more." In that tender exchange, I felt years of hurt melt away. We didn't get to discuss every apology or every detail of the past – there wasn't time for full closure on earthly terms. But in a profound way, God gave us spiritual closure. Our hearts were reconciled, even if all words were not spoken. There was nothing but love between us in those final moments, and that was grace itself. Four months after my divorce, my father passed away from this life and into God's hands. I was there in the hospital room holding his hand as he took his last breath. Of course, I wept – I wept for the goodbye, and for the years that we could have had. But amid the tears, there was a profound sense of completion. I felt an unexpected warmth in my spirit, a reassurance that nothing was lost that wasn't now found in God's mercy. In the days following his death, as I helped plan his funeral and sorted through his belongings, I was struck by the mystery of God's timing. My father's funeral was a celebration of a life that had stumbled and been redeemed in the eleventh hour. I shared during the service about how God had orchestrated healing between us, quoting that promise from Malachi that had become so precious to me: how God "will restore the hearts of the fathers to their children, and the hearts of the children to their fathers,"

Our story was a testament to that very restoration. Even those in attendance who knew how strained things had been were moved by the reconciliation that took place. In the quiet after everyone left, I stood at my father's graveside and whispered a prayer of thanks. I thanked God for using every part of my journey – even the most painful betrayal of my marriage – to bring about this unexpected blessing of healing with my dad. It is a strange thing, but I realized I would endure it all again – the heartbreak, the loneliness – because it led me to this breakthrough of forgiveness and love. What I had with my father at the end was something I feared I'd never have: peace. And not just peace with him, but peace in my own heart. I felt lighter, as if decades-old chains had finally fallen off. The complexity of my father-daughter relationship didn't magically disappear, but it was washed in forgiveness. I acknowledge that not every wound was discussed, not every question answered – yet, there was spiritual restoration that ran deeper than words. I came to understand that sometimes full closure in human terms isn't possible, but God can still give you true closure in your soul. It's the kind of closure where you can remember without bitterness, where love has the last word over loss. God had given me that gift. My father died redeemed in my eyes, and I pray also in God's. And I lived on, not with the old wound gaping, but with a tender scar that told the story of healing. As I write this, reflecting on all that transpired, I am overwhelmed with a sense of peace and gratitude. What began as the darkest chapter of my life – betrayal and divorce – became the catalyst for one of the most beautiful transformations in my life. It humbled me and brought me to the end of myself, only to find God's grace waiting there. I think of Joseph's words to his brothers in Genesis, when he finally forgave them: "You intended to harm me, but God intended it for good." In my case, what the enemy intended for my destruction through betrayal, God turned into an avenue for good, for healing generations of hurt. Truly, He did not waste my pain. I am living proof that "in all things God works for the good of those who love him." Even the things that nearly break us. I also have a renewed understanding of the heart of my Heavenly Father. In reconciling with my earthly dad, I caught a glimpse of the even greater love of God, who never leaves or forsakes His children. When I think about the lonely little girl I once was, I know now that I was never truly fatherless, God was always there, a Father to the fatherless all along guiding my life to this very moment. He filled the gaps my earthly father couldn't fill, and He healed the deepest wound of my heart. As Psalm 147:3 reminds us, *"He heals the brokenhearted and binds up their wounds."* I consider myself a living testament to that promise.

My heart, once fractured by both the first man I ever loved (my dad) and the second man I ever loved (my husband), is now gently bound up by the Lord's own hand. The scars are there, but they are scars of grace. I end this chapter with gratitude. Gratitude for a God who cares so much that He would reopen a wound not to hurt me, but to truly heal me. Gratitude for the precious, if brief, season of reconciliation with my father – a gift I will treasure always. And gratitude for the peace that now permeates my life. I have learned that forgiveness is the doorway to freedom, and that our Heavenly Father can redeem any story – no matter how broken – if we trust Him with the pieces. I miss my dad, but I carry no bitterness, only love. As I move forward, I do so with a heart made whole, ready to embrace the future with hope. In place of the ashes of betrayal, God has given me beauty. In place of mourning, He's given me joy. In place of a spirit of despair, I wear a garment of praise. My journey from betrayal to breakthrough has been painful, yes, but also profoundly sacred. I step into the next chapter of my life with a peace that truly surpasses understanding, and with deep thankfulness that my story, even the hardest parts are held in the hands of a faithful Father who never lets go.

CHAPTER 10

Purpose in the Pain

There comes a moment, after the dust of heartbreak settles, when you realize that survival alone is no longer enough. You want more than just breath in your lungs. You want purpose. Meaning. A reason to believe your pain wasn't wasted.

For me, that moment came when I began asking God, not just to fix what had been broken, but to reveal what He wanted to build through me. The hurt, the silence, the shattered dreams, surely there had to be a reason behind it all. And somewhere between crying in the bathroom at work and standing in worship on Sunday mornings, I began to see a pattern: pain had been pushing me toward purpose all along.

I used to think purpose was reserved for perfect people. People who hadn't gone through a divorce. People whose lives hadn't unraveled publicly. But God kept whispering otherwise. He reminded me that there are broken people all throughout the Bible, and yet He used them; Rahab, the prostitute. David, the adulterer. Paul, the persecutor. And, He gave them purpose.

I began to ask Him: "What do You want to do with my story?" I didn't want my suffering to be for nothing. If I had to walk through the valley, then I wanted to come out carrying someone else's healing in my hands.

This desire didn't erase the pain, but it transformed how I carried it. Instead of hiding my wounds, I started to share them. I told my story to other women. I started journaling more openly. I began volunteering, speaking, even dreaming again. Not because everything was healed, but because I knew God was doing something in me and through me.

Isaiah 61:3 became my anthem: "...to bestow on them a crown of beauty instead of ashes, the oil of joy instead of mourning, and a garment of praise instead of a spirit of despair." I was still standing in the ashes, but I could feel the crown being formed.

Pain, I discovered, is a platform. It draws others closer. It opens hearts. It makes you real. And when you allow God to use it, pain can become a ministry.

I never would have chosen this path. But I wouldn't trade who I'm becoming. Because now, when I meet women going through betrayal, I can look them in the eyes and say, "Me too. And I promise you'll survive this."

Purpose doesn't erase pain. But it does redeem it. And that's what God has been doing all along—redeeming my story.

If you're in the middle of the fire, let me encourage you: God wastes nothing. Not one tear. Not one night. Not one silent scream.

He is using it all to shape something beautiful in you.

There is purpose in your pain.

There is power in your survival.

And there is promise in your becoming.

You are not just a victim of your story. You are a vessel of glory.

Let *Him* write it.

CHAPTER 11

A Sacred Shift

Starting over isn't just a change of address or an updated relationship status. It's not rearranging furniture or altering the contact list in your phone. Starting over is much deeper; it's a transformation of posture. A quiet, sacred shift in how you carry yourself, how you show up in the world, and how you begin to see yourself through God's eyes again.

After the whirlwind of divorce, grief, healing, and revelation, I found myself not just rebuilding a life, I was reintroducing myself to *me*. I wasn't the same woman who once begged to be chosen, who whispered desperate prayers asking someone to come back, to stay, to see her worth. That version of me had died in the fire; and in her place, a stronger, wiser, softer, and yet more powerful woman was emerging. I had come to realize I didn't need to be chosen by anyone else to be worthy. I already *was*. Worthiness wasn't something someone else could give or take, it was something God had sealed within me all along.

Starting over required a kind of courage that had nothing to do with other people. It was about learning to trust others again;

more urgently, it was about trusting *myself.* Trusting my voice, my choices, my discernment. Trusting that the woman rising from the ashes was not a broken version of her former self, but a refined one. A woman being made new.

I began to find joy in the simplest things. I celebrated solo movie nights without feeling lonely. I journaled in the park and didn't feel the need to check my phone. I wandered grocery store aisles slowly, no longer rushing through life. I cooked for one, not with sadness, but with intention. I danced while folding laundry. I prayed out loud in my home with freedom—no longer filtering my prayers, no longer hiding my needs. And slowly, moment by moment, I began to *savor* the life I was creating. One peaceful routine at a time.

Part of starting over meant drawing boundaries I used to feel guilty for. Saying "no" without lengthy explanations. Loving others, yes—but without losing myself in the process. I stopped tying my identity to how much I could endure or how much I could fix. Instead, I stood firm in who I had become—not defined by what I had gone through, but shaped by how I rose from it.

Hebrews 10:35–36 became a truth I clung to: *"So do not throw away your confidence; it will be richly rewarded. You need to persevere so that when you have done the will of God, you will receive what he has promised."* Confidence wasn't about arrogance. It was about knowing who I was in Christ and remembering that God doesn't waste anything, not even the pain. My perseverance had purpose. And there was still promise ahead.

There were moments when doubt crept in—moments I questioned everything, moments I felt that dull ache of loneliness again. But this time, the loneliness was different. It wasn't the ache of rejection or the emptiness of abandonment. It was the quiet loneliness of growth. The still space God sometimes uses to shape us deeper. A space where we shed old skins and embrace new strength. Healing was happening—not perfectly, not on a tidy timeline—but deeply.

And in that healing, I found power. I found my voice in the silence. I found my value in the mirror. I found strength I never knew I had—strength that came not from striving, but from surrendering.

This new chapter of my life isn't about proving anything to anyone. It's not about revenge or rebuilding to show I'm okay. It's about *being*. Being whole. Being seen. Being loved by God, and yes, finally, by *me*.

Starting over didn't mean I erased my past. That would be impossible and honestly, dishonoring. My past mattered because it taught me, refined me, and led me back to myself. I honor that past every time I choose to move forward. Every time I choose hope instead of bitterness. Every time I speak kindly to the woman in the mirror.

If you are standing at the edge of a new beginning, wondering how to begin again—start small. You don't need to have it all figured out. You just need to begin. Start where you are. Start with the next right thing. God doesn't require perfection—He requires surrender. And the beautiful truth is this: *"He will repay you for the years the locusts have eaten"* (Joel 2:25). Nothing is wasted in His hands.

Isaiah 61:3 promises that for those who mourn, He gives *"a crown of beauty instead of ashes, the oil of joy instead of mourning, and a garment of praise instead of a spirit of despair."* I am living proof of that exchange. And Romans 8:28 reminds me that *"in all things God works for the good of those who love Him."* Even this. Especially this.

There's something sacred in starting over. It isn't weakness. It isn't failure. It's holy ground. It's the place where you stop surviving and start living. Where you don't lean on your own understanding anymore, but begin to *trust in the Lord with all your heart* (Proverbs 3:5–6). It's the quiet strength of rising again; this time not just with hope, but with wisdom. With grace.

And here's what I know now:

You are not starting from scratch.
You are starting from *experience.*
And that... is powerful.

CHAPTER 12

Helping My Child Heal

Divorce doesn't just break the marriage; it shakes the whole family. As much as I tried to shield my son from the storm, he still felt the tremors. I'll never forget the day we walked into the house after his father left. Everything looked normal until my son noticed the big screen TV was gone. That was what hit him first. Not the missing clothes. Not the empty closet. But the TV. Children see loss in ways we don't always expect. I sat him down and told him, "This isn't your fault. You didn't do anything wrong. Sometimes marriages don't work out." It broke me to have that conversation, but I knew he needed to hear it from me.

Months later, after the divorce was final, the grief showed up in a bigger way. My son was in third grade when the teacher called me. He had a complete meltdown at school. And I was the school nurse, which meant I was the one who had to comfort him that day. I held him, reassured him again, and told him we would get through this together. But the truth was, I knew this was deeper than just sadness. He was carrying anger, confusion, and fear that I couldn't fix with one hug.

That's when I turned to therapy for him. As parents, we sometimes think love alone will be enough, but professional help was the best decision. My son struggled with weight gain, anger outbursts, and the grief of also losing my dad, his grandfather, all in a short span of time. He was trying to carry too much, too young. Therapy gave him an outlet, and it gave me tools to support him better.

Now, years later, he's in ninth grade and thriving. Sports have been a huge part of his healing. Coaches, uncles, and mentors have stepped in and poured into him when I couldn't do it alone. Weekly check-ins have become our routine; sometimes light, sometimes deep, but always honest. He knows he can come to me, and I make space to ask him, "How are you really doing?" Because even though time has passed, healing is still a process for him.

One of the most powerful moments came when he told me, "Mom, I'm proud of you. You're doing so good." That reminded me that even though children are hurting, they're also watching. They see how we rise, how we cope, and how we model resilience.

So, if you're reading this as a parent walking your child through divorce, here are some ways that helped me — and may help you:

Create a safe space. Keep reminding your child it isn't their fault.

Seek support. Don't be afraid of counseling or therapy. It's not a weakness; it's a tool.

Build a circle. Surround your child with coaches, teachers, family, and mentors who can step in.

Check in regularly. Don't assume they're fine because they're smiling. Ask. Listen.

Let them see healing. It's okay for your child to know you hurt — but also let them see you leaning on God and moving forward.

Divorce leaves scars, but with love, faith, and intentional support, those scars don't have to define our children's future. They can heal, grow, and thrive. Sometimes, they'll even remind us of the strength we didn't know we had.

Prayer

Heavenly Father,

Thank You for entrusting me with the gift of motherhood. I lift up every parent and every child walking through the pain of divorce or family loss. Lord, remind us that healing belongs to You, and that our children are never out of Your reach. Give us wisdom to know when to comfort and when to seek help. Strengthen us to model resilience and faith, even when our hearts are heavy. Surround our children with mentors, coaches, and loved ones who can speak life into them. Protect their minds and guard their hearts. May they always know they are loved, chosen, and safe. And may our homes be places of peace, healing, and hope.

In Jesus' name,

Amen.

CHAPTER 13

Reflecting on the Journey

As I look back over this journey, I see the hand of God in every step, even the ones that felt like breaking. Betrayal opened wounds I never thought I would survive, but it also opened the door to my healing. Divorce shook my foundation, but it also pushed me toward a deeper relationship with the One who never leaves.

There were nights I cried until I had no words left. There were days I fought to simply get out of bed. There were moments I thought my story was over. But God whispered to me that it was only beginning.

Through prayer, therapy, journaling, worship, travel nursing, and even stepping on a bodybuilding stage, I found myself again. I learned that healing is not neat or linear. It is messy, raw, and requires courage. But it is possible.

And now, as I approach my 50th birthday, I can honestly say I am not just surviving, I am thriving. I have so many plans ahead, not just for myself, but for the women around me who need to know that life does not end with heartbreak. I want my story to be an inspiration and motivation, a reminder that yes, life is hard and heavy, but with God and with the right outlets, you don't have to carry it alone.

I am still thriving as a nurse. I still love on my children and my family. I am living with purpose, with joy, and with hope. I may carry scars, but I also carry strength; and both are proof of God's faithfulness.

Today, I stand stronger. I laugh again. I live with freedom. I have learned that I don't have to be defined by what broke me. Instead, I am defined by the God who restored me.

And to you, the one holding this book, know this: You will not always feel this broken. You will not always cry this hard. You will not always carry this weight.

Your breakthrough is coming. It may not look like mine, but God has a way of turning ashes into beauty, pain into purpose, endings into new beginnings.

"See, I am doing a new thing! Now it springs up; do you not perceive it? I am making a way in the wilderness and streams in the wasteland." (Isaiah 43:19, NIV)

This is not the end of your story.

It is the beginning of your breakthrough.

Scripture Reflections

Listed below are a few scriptures that spoke to me throughout my journey, I pray they speak to you just as they have spoken to me:

...to bestow on them a crown of beauty instead of ashes, the oil of joy instead of mourning, and a garment of praise instead of a spirit of despair.

Isaiah 61:3 (NIV)

And we know that in all things God works for the good of those who love him, who have been called according to his purpose.

Romans 8:28 (NIV)

The Lord is close to the brokenhearted and saves those who are crushed in spirit.

Psalm 34:18 (NIV)

So do not throw away your confidence; it will be richly rewarded. You need to persevere so that when you have done the will of God, you will receive what he has promised.

Hebrews 10:35-36 (NIV)

But he said to me, 'My grace is sufficient for you, for my power is made perfect in weakness.' Therefore, I will boast all the more gladly about my weaknesses, so that Christ's power may rest on me.

2 Corinthians 12:9 (NIV)

Trust in the Lord with all your heart and lean not on your own understanding; in all your ways submit to him, and he will make your paths straight.

Proverbs 3:5-6 (NIV)

I will repay you for the years the locusts have eaten...

Joel 2:25 (NIV)

'For I know the plans I have for you,' declares the Lord, 'plans to prosper you and not to harm you, plans to give you hope and a future.'

Jeremiah 29:11 (NIV)

Reflections:
Your Journey to Wholeness

After the Breaking: Facing the Pain

Questions:

- What moment in your story felt like your breaking point?

- How have you been trying to carry the weight of grief, responsibility, or shame?

- What emotions have you been avoiding, and why?

- What are you still trying to fix that God may be asking you to release?

- In what ways have you been asking God to change someone else—when He's been trying to change you?

Encouragement:

"The Lord is close to the brokenhearted and saves those who are crushed in spirit."

(Psalm 34:18)

You don't have to pretend you're okay. God does His best work in the pieces.

In the Stillness: Discovering Yourself Again

Questions:

- When was the last time you were truly still—emotionally, spiritually, mentally?

- What have you learned about yourself in solitude?

- What does healing look like for *you*, personally?

- What "noise" is God asking you to turn down in your life?

- Are there areas of your heart where God is still whispering truth over shame?

Encouragement:

> *"Be still and know that I am God."*
> *(Psalm 46:10)*

Stillness is not a setback. It's sacred space for transformation.

Rebuilding: With Intention and Identity

Questions:

- Who are you now, compared to who you were before the heartbreak?

- What lies about your worth or identity have you been believing?

- What boundaries do you need to establish to protect your peace?

- What brings you joy—true, deep, soul-level joy?

- How is your life reflecting your values, not just your wounds?

Encouragement:

"She is clothed with strength and dignity, and she laughs without fear of the future."

(Proverbs 31:25)

You are not a victim of your story. You are the vessel through which God is writing something beautiful.

Moving Forward: With Grace and Wisdom

Questions:

- What does "starting over" mean to you right now?

- What would it look like to fully forgive—others, yourself, and even God?

- What does trusting God look like in your current season?

- How can you celebrate the woman you've become?

- What dream or desire are you afraid to pursue because of past pain?

Encouragement:

"I will repay you for the years the locusts have eaten."
(Joel 2:25)

Nothing is wasted. God is in the business of divine recovery.

Becoming: Not Who You Were, But Who You're Called to Be

Questions:

- Who is the woman God is calling you to be in this next season?

- How will you continue to show up for yourself daily?

- What spiritual truths do you need to keep speaking over your life?

- How can your pain serve someone else's healing?

- What would you say to the past version of you—and what do you want to say to the future you?

Encouragement:

"For I know the plans I have for you," declares the Lord, "plans to prosper you and not to harm you, plans to give you hope and a future."
(Jeremiah 29:11)

You are not starting over from nothing. You are starting over with *everything* God has taught you.

Helping Others Heal: The Heart of the Child

Questions:

- How can I create a safe, open space for my child to express their feelings about loss or change?

- Who can I invite into my child's circle of support — mentors, family, teachers, or coaches?

- In what ways can I model healing and faith so my child sees resilience in action?

Encouragement:

"Start children off on the way they should go, and even when they are old they will not turn from it."

(Proverbs 22:6, NIV)

Final Journal Prompt:

Write a letter to yourself:

- A letter to your **past self**: the woman who didn't know she'd make it.

- A letter to your **present self**: the woman who's still standing.

- A letter to your **future self**: the woman who's walking into freedom, peace, and purpose.

Closing Prayer

Heavenly Father,

Thank You for being a God of restoration, a God who binds up the brokenhearted and calls beauty from ashes. I lift every woman, every reader walking through heartbreak, transition, or uncertainty. Remind them they are never alone. Remind them that starting over is not a punishment, but a divine invitation.

Give them the strength to rise, the grace to release, and the courage to believe in joy again. Wrap them in peace that surpasses understanding. Renew their hope, revive their hearts, and restore their purpose.

May their pain birth power.

May their sorrow birth strength.

And may their story bring You glory.

In Jesus' name,

Amen.

Epilogue
From Broken to Beautiful

You've walked with me through heartbreak, healing, prayer, silence, and rediscovery. If you're holding this book and still turning pages, it means you made it through some of your hardest moments too. Or maybe you're still in the middle of them—bleeding, but breathing.

Wherever you are, I want to remind you of something: **This is not where your story ends.** Yes, the marriage ended. Yes, the pain was real. Yes, the prayers didn't always get answered the way you hoped.

But even after the loss… there is **life**. And that's what the next book is all about. It's not about divorce. It's about **what comes after**.

The quiet after the storm. The rediscovery of your voice. The surprising joy that rises from places you thought were dead. The confidence to make decisions without second-guessing yourself. The power of creating a life not marked by survival, but by *wholeness*.

From Broken to Beautiful is for the woman who has taken off the wedding ring, but still wears the weight of her past.

For the mother trying to raise strong children while healing a wounded heart. For the woman of faith who still believes God is good, even when the story didn't go the way she planned. It's for the woman who wants to laugh again, love again, and truly live again.

- In this next book we' will talk about:
- Dating after divorce (and when *not* to)
- Finding purpose in singleness
- Healing your body and your self-image
- Parenting while healing
- Boundaries that honor your growth
- And trusting God in a brand-new season

The next book isn't just a continuation of this one. It's a *becoming*. A bold, brave, Spirit-led becoming. Because you weren't just broken—you were *rebuilt*. And the woman you're becoming? She is powerful. She is peaceful. She is whole.

So, if you're wondering what life looks like on the other side of heartbreak… If you're asking, "Can I really begin again?" The answer is yes.

Yes, you can.

And I'd be honored to walk with you into the next part of the journey.

About the Author

Wanna Perkins is a nurse, wellness coach, mother, and now, published author. With over two decades of experience in healthcare and a heart rooted in faith, Wanna has devoted her life to caring for others, both physically and spiritually.

Her journey through heartbreak, healing, and self-discovery has inspired her to share her story with transparency and truth. As a mother of two sons, a competitive bodybuilder, and a woman of unshakable resilience, Wanna knows what it means to rise from the ashes.

Wanna is passionate about empowering women to find their strength, rebuild their faith, and walk boldly in their worth. She believes healing is possible for anyone willing to surrender, reflect, and grow.

When she's not working or writing, Wanna can be found listening to sermons, dancing in the kitchen, or mentoring others through fitness and faith. She currently resides in Texas and continues to serve her community through nursing, speaking, and storytelling.

Connect with Wanna:

Email: wannaperkins24@gmail.com

Instagram: @wanna_be_well and @its_me_wannamonic

More books coming soon…

www.ingramcontent.com/pod-product-compliance
Lightning Source LLC
Chambersburg PA
CBHW072045040426
42447CB00012BB/3027